Quick Guide to your Career in Transcription

Liz Broomfield

ISBN: 1508587701
978-1508587705

DEDICATION

To Matthew and to my lovely transcription clients who
helped me to learn all that I know.

CONTENTS

ACKNOWLEDGEMENTS

I thank my husband, my colleagues and my customers, and all of the readers who have enjoyed the e-book so far and those who asked for a print edition.

INTRODUCTION

Welcome to this quick guide to transcription as a career.

It's quick because it aims to give you all of the information to get up and running in as short a space as possible. But it's packed with information and insights on how to get started as a transcriber, tricks of the trade, and more general information about working as a freelancer and getting jobs.

I've been working as a transcriber since 2010, although I originally trained in audio-typing back in 1993! I got my very first transcription job via Twitter (and I'll share some hints about how to do that later on, as I believe it's a very good way to get transcription work in particular), when a music journalist who I followed asked if anyone knew of a good transcriber. "I've done audio-typing", I thought, "How hard can it be?" So I pitched for and got the job, transcribing an interview with a rock star (ooh!) … and had a bit of a time of it.

I didn't know what technology to use to control my tape – I didn't even know that there WAS special technology. So I ran the tape through Windows Media Player and clicked into that window every time I wanted to stop it. No pedals here, and no tape player, either! I didn't' really know how to use Autocorrect to my advantage … I was basically all at sea in a mass of inefficiency – and I certainly wish that I'd had somebody to advise me!

Since then, I've built up the transcription side of my business to include more music journalists, political journalists, individual entrepreneurs who need transcripts of podcasts and agencies that produce conference reports. I've built up a dual specialism in people who are speaking non-native English and those musicians (a surprising number of larger agencies don't like tapes with swearing etc. on them – I'm not bothered by that, so I've carved out a niche for myself there). I don't do it full time, as I'm also an editor, proofreader and localiser, but it's certainly an important – and enjoyable – part of my business.

In this guide, I'm going to share with you …

- What transcription actually is
- Why human transcribers are still necessary (useful information for yourself and for prospective clients!)
- How to work out whether you're suited for transcription
- How to build your skills
- How to actually work as a professional transcriber

I'm also going to give you some tools for making transcription quicker and more efficient, mainly centring around using AutoCorrect in Word. Then, at the end, the appendices will give you some useful tips on setting up as a freelancer and ways to get freelance work.

I really hope that you enjoy this book and find it useful. PLEASE post a review wherever you bought it, blog about it and spread the word. As an independent publisher, I don't have the force of a marketing department behind me, and all of the online book websites use reviews and ratings to calculate who they show books to and how they promote them, so every review and share and mention really helps!

If you want to get in touch with me, do drop me a

line at liz@libroediting.com or via the website www.libroediting.com. I love hearing from my readers!

WHAT IS TRANSCRIPTION?

Basically, transcription involves listening to a recording of something and typing the contents up into a document, which is then returned to the client, giving them a written record of what's on the recording. Typically, this will be an interview – which might be something a journalist has undertaken with someone they're writing about, or part of a study, where a researcher has interviewed subjects and needs to record their responses. It can take absolutely ages to type out a recording like this – much longer than you think it will, particularly if you don't type very fast!

When I learnt to audio-type, it was all done with tapes and a special pedal you pressed to play and rewind the recording. These days, although you can still get the pedals, it can all be done with MP3s, some special software (I use the paid version of NCH ExpressScribe[1] – they do also offer a free version) and the function keys on the keyboard take the place of the pedals. You can even speed up or slow down the playback.

The time it takes to transcribe a recording depends on several factors:

> the speed at which the people are talking

> the number of people talking

> the clarity of the recording (background noise, phone interview …)

> the clarity of the speaking voices (accents, speaking English as a second language, mumbling …)

---

[1] www.nch.com.au/scribe/index.html

WHY YOU NEED TO BE HUMAN TO PRODUCE A GOOD TRANSCRIPTION

When I receive a recording for a new transcription client and tell them I've loaded it into my transcription management software, I'm sometimes asked if that does the transcribing for me. Um, no.

While there are of course software packages out there that are very good at working with a single voice dictating, even those can sometimes struggle. I know this, because I've edited work that has been dictated in this way – and it can often be rife with homophones.

Why use a human transcriber?

I've been providing transcription services for several years now. While a machine might be suitable for taking down the words of a single, non-accented speaker enunciating clearly into a good quality recording apparatus, with no background noise, no interruptions and no acronyms or jargon, the projects I've worked on have included some or all of these features:

High levels of background noise – interviews in cafes with espresso machines whooshing and spoons clinking in cups

People talking while they're eating and eating while they're talking

Interruptions from waiters / room service / other members of the band or group

High levels of tape noise leaving me straining to hear what anyone's saying

Multiple speakers including many people with similar voices around a conference table

Overlapping speech

Non-native English accents or heavy regional accents

Very technical content – jargon and acronyms galore

Creative content – album names, track names, novel titles, band names, author names

Requests to provide the transcription missing out ums and ers through to smoothing the English to make it read as standard English

As a native English speaker specialising in working with music journalists and non-native speakers of English, I can cope with all of these, with some rewinding and checking. I doubt that the most sophisticated dictation software could do so, as yet. I might be wrong of course (let me know if I am!).

Understanding what's being said on a transcription

The first issue is actually hearing and understanding what's being said. I have a good ear and a native English speaker's ability to predict what will come next in a sentence / how sentence structures work, plus my experience working with speakers of and texts in non-native English allows me to do this for native Arabic, Chinese, Eastern European language etc. speakers. My ear can filter out background noise where sophisticated software can only go so far. And I can hear around the clink of teaspoons or glasses chinking to grasp what's being said.

Checking the content in a transcription

When one of my journalist clients sends me a tape, I check who the musician / band is and look them up (usually on Wikipedia for the general information, as their own websites are usually a bit harder to plumb for information). When I'm working on an international conference I will seek out or be given a conference schedule, list of attendees, etc. When I'm working with technical content I will look up information on that topic.

All this allows me to produce a transcription which the client will not have to check for themselves, or if they do check it (which I do recommend), there won't be too much to change. And I won't be embarrassed by too many mis-hearings. Just try popping a few names of country leaders, bands or albums into a Word document and running a spell checker and imagine what an automated dictation program would do with these terms!

Speech on a tape to words in a document

Very occasionally I'll be asked to record exactly what the people on the tape say, including ums, ahs, repetitions and pauses. At the moment, I'm transcribing some roleplays for students learning how to operate a telephone helpline. Here it's important to capture all the nuances of the conversation and I'm splitting the utterances into sections, numbering them, and including all the ums and ahs.

Normally, my clients will require some smoothing out.

Most of my journalists like to have an indication of when their subject slowed down or had to mull over something and ask me to include notes of those pauses.

Business people producing podcasts and telecasts often want a fairly accurate transcription, but smoothed out to eliminate ums, ahs, pauses and repetitions, so they have a good product to sell or include in packages for their clients.

Some international conferences want to avoid embarrassment for their delegates by having their English rewritten as I transcribe to appear as close as possible to native British (or American) English

I have worked with authors who start off with a tape and want it to turn into something they can publish as a book (this, unlike all of the other options, involves two processes: transcription and then heavy editing and rewriting).

Why should people use a human transcriber and not a software program?

I think I've answered that for you now. Your clients should also consider using a human transcriber who's a native speaker of the language that they're having transcribed: there are websites out there where you can find very cheap transcribers; they are often not going to be native English speakers and while they will get the gist of the tape down, I'd be unsure whether they could give them the service that they needed..

HOW DO YOU START A CAREER IN TRANSCRIPTION?

Here are some pointers to give you an idea of what you need to know in advance, the skills and software you need, and ways to get work in this field – plus some pitfalls to avoid.

What is transcription?

I covered this in detail earlier in this guide, but basically transcription is what we used to call audio-typing – turning recordings of spoken words into documents containing those words written down. There is quite a lot of call for transcription work of various kinds, as we'll see in a moment. But the work basically involves putting on a headset or ear phones, and typing out what you can hear on a tape.

What kinds of transcription job are available?

Personally, I've worked on the following kinds of transcription job, which just shows how varied it can be:

Journalists interviewing musicians and actors

Someone interviewing their elderly parent in order to write a memoir for them

Academics and students interviewing subjects for their research

Students' role-plays for learning how to provide phone counselling

Presentations at international conferences

Panels at conferences including questions

Discussion panels for market research companies

Podcasts by one person so they can provide transcriptions to their listeners

Podcasts of one person interviewing another

Free and paid-for telecasts (phone-in sessions where people listen to a speaker)

Free and paid-for teleseminars (as above but with questions and discussion)

Content for a book, dictated in the first instance before being edited

There are also specific roles that people can take on who have particular specialised skills such as legal proceedings or letters and medical transcription.

All of these clients have had different requirements in terms of the level of detail, time stamping, etc. but all have provided variety and interest!

Am I suited for transcription work?

In essence, the answer comes down to these three points:

1. How fast do you type? You need to be able to type really fast to be able to make enough money (see below)
2. How careful are you with your posture? (sounds odd, but sitting in one position typing like mad for hours is the highest risk part of my job for RSI)
3. How good are you at using Word and its autocorrect features? (this makes a lot of difference to your speed – see the section on

> technology below and the chapters entitled
> Tools later on)

The best way to find out if you're suitable for this kind of work is to practise before you're doing a paid job.

Learn from me, here! I did train as an audio typist, with a foot pedal and a tape player back in the old days. So when a journalist who I followed on Twitter asked if anyone offered transcription, I went for and got the job. Fine, I did lovely fast typing but I was using Windows Media Player to play the tape, switching windows to start, pause and rewind it. That first tape took me hours! I wish I'd known what I know now about technology and how to actually do it!

Technology for transcription work

There's quite a lot to the technology for transcription, so do read on to the chapter below on working as a professional transcriber, which includes loads of detail on this and other aspects.

In essence, you will need:

> a word-processing package
>
> software to manage your recordings
>
> ways to receive large files – you need to know

about Dropbox, Hightail and other services

How do I work out if I'm suitable for transcription work?

If anyone asks me about how to find out if they're suitable for transcription work I tell them to do this:

Record an hour of general conversation, interviews, etc. from the radio

Get the technology set up (see separate article) and transcribe it

Work out how many minutes it takes you to transcribe one audio minute

I'd say you're looking for at least a 1:3 relationship here. That's 3 minutes to transcribe one minute of tape. Not long! you cry. But that means it will take 45 minutes to transcribe a 15-minute tape, or 3 hours to transcribe a 1-hour tape. Build in the fact that you need to take a break at least once an hour, and good old cash rears its ugly head.

Can I make money doing transcription?

Here's the thing it all boils down to:

If you can't type fast and use the technology to boost your speed, it's not financially worthwhile to take on transcription work.

The standard industry rate for transcription is around £0.85 per audio minute. That's £8.50 for a 10-minute file. If it takes you 1 hour to type out a 10-minute file, you're going to make £8.50. Before tax. But if you can get two of those done in an hour, you're getting £17.00 an hour – not so bad.

Some clients have standard rates and pay a bit more than that – that's usually for specialised work, though. It's always worth asking their rates before you proffer yours, however!

Personally, I stick to that rate for one to two speakers speaking clear English in a relatively quiet room, with a turnaround time that allows me some room for manoeuvre, and I add £0.10 per minute for urgent work, each extra speaker, noisy tapes, etc. And if any of my music journalist clients are reading this, yes, I give fellow freelancers a discount (and other people a discount at my discretion, based on the quality of the tapes and the time it takes me to transcribe them).

There are internet job boards out there trying to hire transcribers for £0.10 per audio minute – honestly. The more people accept these prices, the more they will stay. I have more self-worth than that, and even when I was starting out, I'd rather do a transcription for free in return for a reference than do hack work for a corporation paying peanuts. Rant over!

How do I get transcription work?

There are loads of sources of transcription work. I have to say that my main one is personal recommendation – strings of journalists, etc. But it's also worth trying the following:

Set up a saved Twitter search for "need transcriber" and contact people with an offer. This can work – it's how I got my first transcription client!

If you are near a university that has a lot of research going on, ask to put up some posters offering your services. A lot of researchers conduct interviews and need them to be transcribed.

If you already offer other services and are adding transcription to your roster, tell your editing or other clients that you're offering this new service – I've transitioned clients to and from transcription services.

Join reputable job sites like Proz which advertise transcription jobs at decent prices.

Use social media and tell all your contacts what you're doing

Join transcribers' groups on LinkedIn, etc. – there are often people looking to pass on overflow work

I would strongly suggest that you don't just do transcription work full time. It's very physically tiring, you can get RSI from all the typing and sore ears from the earphones (I've got a sore ear at the moment and I've been doing this for years!) so add it into the mix, and remember to take a break every hour of typing!

Next, we're going to talk about the nitty-gritty of professional transcription technology..

WORKING AS A PROFESSIONAL TRANSCRIBER

In this section, we're going to go into more detail about the technology you can use to help you, and how to produce a professional transcription that will bring you repeat and recommended business.

Technology for transcription work

The first thing you need is a word-processing package, of course. I use Microsoft Word.

Then you need some software to manage your recordings. I use NCH ExpressScribe.

It's also a good idea to sign up to (the free options of) services like Dropbox and Hightail, and to be aware of these services, as the audio files people will want to send you might well be very large – too large to send by email attachment.

Why do I need to use transcription software?

When I mention transcription software, some people think I sneakily use special software to do the actual transcription! Not at all! What ExpressScribe does is allow me to

a) manage my transcriptions – I load all the ones I have to do into the software and I can see how long they are and keep my place in them. As I complete them, I delete them from the software (they'll still be in my files on my PC, though).

b) manage aspects of the tape like the loudness and speed of the tape (if people are talking really slowly, I can speed the tape up slightly and get through it more quickly)

c) start, stop, rewind and fast forward the tapes using the function keys on my keyboard (or any other keys I choose to assign – I messed around with this a bit and did move one function key that I kept hitting by accident, causing the tape to slow to 50% speed!). You can connect the software to a USB foot pedal if you need to save keyboard movements and use your feet to stop and start the tape.

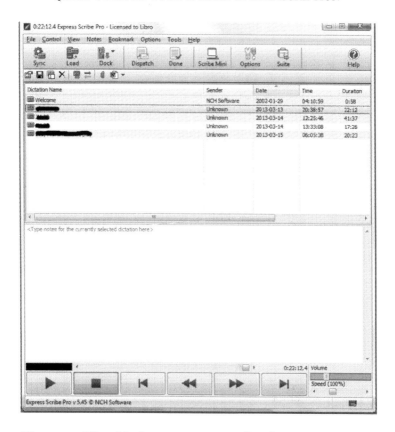

How can Word help me to transcribe faster?

The way Word can really help you is through the use of shortcuts or AutoCorrects. You can find more detailed information about how to use AutoCorrect in the Tools section coming up next.

Basically, you need to get good at:

> Identifying commonly used words or phrases, especially
>
>> longer sets of words or phrases
>> words that you stumble over typing, however short
>
> Assigning keyboard shortcuts to them that you can remember when you're typing

In this way, you can type something like:

"v imp to give envl pons to all ppl in the group to save the env."

and have Word turn that into:

"Very important to give environmental responsibility to people in the group to save the environment."

I've saved almost 50% of the keystrokes needed to type that sentence there, which does build up over the course of 20 pages of transcription!

How can people send me big audio files to transcribe?

Your clients have four options for sending you their audio files. You'll just be sending nice, neat Word documents back, but their files might be enormous!

Option 1 - An ftp server – this looks scary but is used by some of the larger corporates I work with. They will place the audio files on their own server. You will log in and download the file onto your own computer, then either upload the transcription or email it to your contact.

Option 2 - Zipping – this will work for small files but a huge .wav file will still be too large for this method. Your client should be able to right click on the file in their own Windows Explorer (or Mac equivalent) and choose "Send to zip file". This will make the file small enough to send. You will need to unzip it at your end – download the file, right click in Windows Explorer and choose "Extract".

Option 3 - File sharing – a file and folder sharing service like Dropbox will allow your client to save their file in a special folder that can be shared with your email address. Dropbox acts like another folder on your system, and means that you can access the file and save it into your transcription software from the shared folder. You need to have Dropbox installed yourself before you do this but you can get a free version.

Option 4 - Download services – there are millions of these around, but I usually recommend Hightail[2] as I've found that easy to use and reliable. Here, the client uploads their file to the service, enters your email address and the service emails you a link from which to download the document. Watch out, as many of these have a time limit, so get it downloaded as soon as you know it's there! I have an account with Hightail for sending large files, but most of these do not require you to have an account, and the client should be able to send up to a certain file size for free.

All of these options have advantages and disadvantages. Many of my clients know what to use, but some need advising, so it's worth being aware of the options. For options 1 and 4, it's worth waiting a little while from when the client tells you they're uploading the file, as it can take a while to get up onto the server and back to you, so if you're too eager to download, you might end up with half a file!

Producing a professional transcription

I have many regular transcription clients and they recommend me on to their friends and colleagues at a remarkable rate, too. I've asked them what differentiates me from other transcribers, and it

[2] www.hightail.com

comes down to this:

I check the client's requirements up front

I produce an extremely accurate transcription

I produce a transcription with time stamps and other features to make it easy for the client to work with the text

of course, I'm also super-reliable and always set appropriate expectations, but that's part of being a good freelancer, not specific to transcription.

Establishing client requirements

It's important to establish what the client wants out of their transcription right from the start. I will always send my clients a list of questions. These include:

Do you want time stamping every 5 or 10 minutes, or at all? (as in, I type 05:00, 10:00 at the relevant places in the document to indicate those points on the tape)

Do you want me to record every single word, pause, um and er / smooth out the worst bits / rewrite the text in clear English?

Do you want American or English spellings?

Do you need your questions to be written out in full or just in note form (for journalists and researchers)

Do you have any other requirements – questions in Italics, speakers' names in a particular format (for conferences) etc.

Do you have a list of conference attendees and session / paper titles (for conferences)

Once I've established these, I will make a note of them and obey them!

Being accurate

Your client is paying you to take down what's on the audio file for them. Often they won't be able to check the whole thing. I believe it's important to:

Listen carefully and take down the words as accurately as you can

Look up band names, place names, company names and other things they mention

If you can't hear something, don't guess – make a note (see below)

Read through the transcription when you've completed it

Run a spell check over the document when you've finished

I do also warn my clients that any company names, brands, album titles etc. may not be accurate and should be checked. You can't check everything. But you can make sure you spell that village in Somerset or Kazakhstan correctly (if you can't type Kazakhstan quickly, create a shortcut!).

Making your transcription as professional as possible

It's relatively easy to provide a professional transcription that will please and impress your client.

Give the transcription a sensible title and file name

Type it out clearly using a clear font and a fairly large size

If people are talking in great slabs of text, divide it up into paragraphs at natural breaks

Mark time stamps at 5 or 10 minute intervals – new line, 05:00, new line, carry on the text (with no capital if it's half way through a sentence)

Mark places you can't hear like this: insert a note in square brackets with the time of the unclear section: [unclear 32:44] (unless the client requests a different format – I have one who prefers <unclear 32:44>

If the audio file is 50 minutes long and there's a 5 minute gap while the interviewee goes off to answer the phone, or it finishes at 45:30 and then all you can hear is your journalist putting the phone down, sighing and typing, only charge for the audio you transcribed. It's a nice and ethical touch.

Now that we've discussed the technology, I'm going to share some hints and tips about the transcriber's friend: AutoCorrect in Word..

TOOLS 1: USING AUTOCORRECT IN WORD, WHAT IT IS AND WHERE TO FIND IT

Have you come across AutoCorrect yet? Open up a Word document and type "teh". Did it magically change to "the" in front of your eyes? That's AutoCorrect.

So, it's great for correcting common typing mistakes that lots of people make. But did you know that you can harness its power to help you write and type more efficiently and faster? In this article, I'll tell you more about AutoCorrect and explain where to find it in different versions of Word, so you can tinker with it to tailor it to your requirements. I'll explain all that in the next section. For now, let's look at how to access AutoCorrect in the various versions of Word.

Note: there are screen shots to go with these instructions, however they don't come across very well on the Kindle. I link to the original blog post below, where you can see all of the screen shots. But if you don't want to do that, drop me an email and I'll be happy to send you a free pdf of this document for you to read on your tablet or computer.

How to access AutoCorrect in Word 2003

Let's look at Word 2003 first. You can find AutoCorrect under the Tools screen (I have to admit that it was so much better when it was so accessible, right here off a main menu. Nowadays, they like to hide it!). Click on Tools and then near the bottom, you'll find AutoCorrect Options.

Once you've clicked on AutoCorrect Options, you'll find yourself at the AutoCorrect screen. This is where you can see what is already set up, and delete / change / add AutoCorrect entries as you wish. More about that in the next article!

How to access AutoCorrect in Word 2007

When I first moved over to Word 2007, I found it a

bit hard to track down AutoCorrect – the key is to click on that Office button in the top left corner of the screen. When you do that, a menu will come up below the button, with a list of the files you've recently accessed a list of things you can do and, right at the bottom, a Word Options button. Click that button.

Once you have clicked on the Word Options button, you're confronted with another menu (oh, for the simplicity of Word 2003!). Click on Proofing and you will get a menu including the heading AutoCorrect Options. Click on the AutoCorrect Options button …

How to access AutoCorrect in Word 2010 and Word 2013

Now, in Word 2010 I feel like they've buried AutoCorrect just that one level deeper. But we'll find it! To access AutoCorrect in Word 2010 or 2013, you need to first click on that File tab, one to the left of Home, to which Word defaults. This has replaced the Office button from Word 2007. Anyway, Click on the File tab and you will be given a menu which, handily enough, doesn't have a "Word Options" entry, but just Options. Click on Options.

Once you have clicked on Options, you will be given a new menu. This is quite similar to the one in Word

2007. Choose **Proofing** and then **AutoCorrect Options**.

Note that you can also set up a shortcut button on your Quick Access Toolbar if you use this a lot (see section below). Here is your AutoCorrect dialogue box:

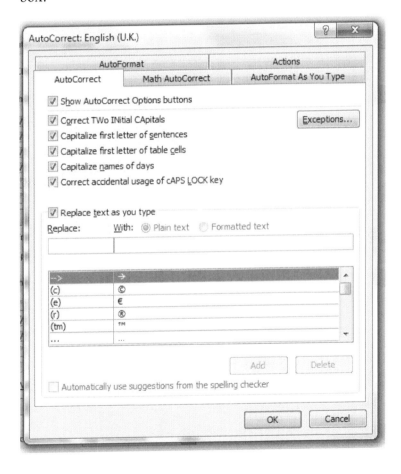

How to access AutoCorrect in Word for Mac

To access AutoCorrect in Word for Mac, choose Tools and then AutoCorrect. Click on the Auto Text tab in the AutoCorrect Preferences dialogue box, and off you go!

For full sets of screenshots guiding you through these processes, please read my online guide.[3]

Adding an Autocorrect button to the Quick Access Toolbar

Note: there are screen shots to go with these instructions, however they don't come across very well on the Kindle. I link to the original blog post below, where you can see all of the screen shots. But if you don't want to do that, drop me an email and I'll be happy to send you a free pdf of this document for you to read on your tablet or computer.

The example I'm going to use is AutoCorrect Options. AutoCorrect is buried within some nested menus, which means you have to click and click and click whenever you want to add a new entry, wasting time to do something in order to save time. Now, I can access the menu I want with just one click!

---

[3] www.libroediting.com/2012/05/23/autocorrect-in-word-1/

So, first of all we need to go up to the **Quick Access Toolbar,** right at the top of your screen in Word 2007, 2010 and 2013 (in Word 2003, right click on the main toolbar and customise it). Note the **down arrow** to the right of your standard buttons, and click it.

You will notice an option to choose **More Commands** – this is how you add more buttons to the Quick Access Toolbar. Click on that, and you'll get a screen which allows you to **customize the Quick Access Toolbar**.

Note at this point that you can access this menu via **Word Options – Customize**, too, if you want to.

We can now see a whole load of **Popular Buttons** you can add on to the Quick Access Toolbar – so you can pop them on there to get at them whenever you want to. These are a few buttons that appear at the top level when you click on any of the tabs on your main ribbon.

We're going deeper, though, into buttons and commands which **don't appear on the top level** of your tab menus. So click on the **arrow** next to Popular Commands and you'll get a list of options.

You can choose **All Commands**, which will give you every command and button (with a hover-over tip to which menu they belong to so you can choose, for example, **Spell Check** from the Review tab rather than the Blog version, which won't do much for you in a standard Word document. In this case, to add our deeply buried button, we want to choose **Commands not on the Ribbon**.

Now you have a list of every command and button that exists in Word. How handy that AutoCorrect begins with an A! Look for your button and highlight it, then click on **Add >>** to add it to the list on the right – which is the list of buttons that appear on your Quick Access Toolbar. At this point you can even choose when these buttons will appear, but I always leave it on **All documents**. When you've pressed **Add**, there it is, on the list.

Click on OK and it will magically appear on your **Quick Access Toolbar**. Want to check it's true? Click on the little icon, and there's our familiar AutoCorrect menu.

What a time saver! I've also added all my **very commonly used buttons from different menus** onto my Quick Access Toolbar, from Bold to Spellcheck and all sorts of other things in between …

Quick method

If you have the button you want to add to the QAT in front of you, simply right click on that button and you will get the option to add it to the quick access toolbar!

Magic! And it works however deeply buried the button is in your lists of commands – for example, you can choose something that appears in a menu within a menu!

You can access all of the screenshots for this article by visiting the original post on my blog.[4]

---

[4] www.libroediting.com/2012/06/27/adding-shortcuts-to-the-quick-access-toolbar/

TOOLS 2: WHY AND HOW TO USE AUTOCORRECT

Now we know how to access AutoCorrect, and basically what it does, we're going to look at how you can use AutoCorrect to **speed up** your typing and make it **more efficient**, and how you actually **amend the AutoCorrect entries** to tailor them to your requirements.

Note: there are screen shots to go with these instructions, however they don't come across very well on the Kindle. I link to the original blog post below, where you can see all of the screen shots. But if you don't want to do that, drop me an email and I'll be happy to send you a free pdf of this document for you to read on your tablet or computer.

Why would I use AutoCorrect?

Apart from correcting common typos, AutoCorrect has **two** very handy uses: I use it in these ways all the time, and if you, you will save yourself time and effort.

If there is **a word you can never remember how to spell**, set up a short cut AutoCorrect, just type in the first few letters, and AutoCorrect will auto complete it for you. No more finding it in the spell checker yet again. Type in **Kaz** and Word will display **Kazakhstan**.

If there is **a long word or particularly a phrase that you use over and over again** – "Creative and Marketing Director", "economic forecasting", "qualitative and quantitative research methodologies", set up a short cut for each one and save all that typing (and possible typos). Type **cmd**, **ef** or **qq** and watch the phrases type themselves!

How do I tailor AutoCorrect to my individual requirements?

The key to this is in the AutoCorrect menu we met last time.

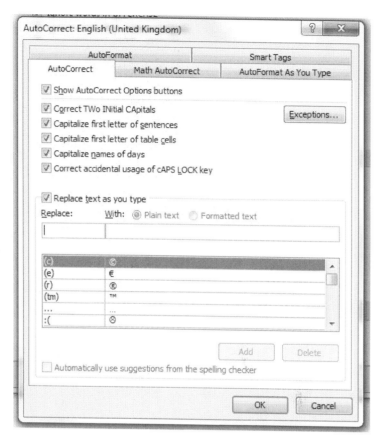

First of all, there are some useful features on the screen directly in front of you. Here's how you turn on and off all those **useful features that sort out typing errors as you go** (we've all typed **THe** at the beginning of a sentence, haven't we). You just untick the box if you don't want it to do something.

So, for now, we're working with the standard

AutoCorrect. We've started off with a list of signs and symbols, because they come before "A" in Word's alphabet. To see what else there is, try **typing a letter** into the top, blank fields. Here we have a mixture of the standard AutoCorrect entries (**abouta** changes to **about**, etc.) but the top two are my own additional entries. See how many keystrokes and how much time I save by typing **aaa** and getting **accountability agent application** inserted into my document (plus it's typed correctly first time!).

How to add a new entry to AutoCorrect

Let's look at how to **add those new, personalised AutoCorrect entries**. Well, it's pretty simple. Type the abbreviation or mis-spelling in the left hand column (or field), the text that you want to appear in the document in the right hand field (or highlight the word you want to add an entry for in your document, then access this menu), and press **Add**.

You can see that your entry has now appeared on the AutoCorrect list, in its place in the alphabetical order. For example, if I put lb in **Replace** and Liz Broomfield in **With**, whenever I type **lb**, the words **Liz Broomfield** will appear in my document.

How to delete an AutoCorrect entry

What if you want to **delete an AutoCorrect entry**? I did this recently – I had set **re** to AutoCorrect to **recognize** for a document I was working on that had no contractions (they're, etc.). Of course, when I was then typing something more informal, I typed lots of **they're** and got lots of **they'recognize** as it tried to do what I'd asked it to do. So I wanted to get rid of that entry altogether. Here's how you do that: **Look up the entry** by typing in your abbreviation – what you type as opposed to what you want to come up. When you've found the one you want to delete, press the **Delete** button.

Note: it doesn't ask you if you're sure you want to delete, but it does leave that entry in the top text fields, so if you've made a mistake, you can just add it again.

How to change or replace an AutoCorrect entry

You may want to **change an AutoCorrect entry** – for example, you're stopping talking about Liz Broomfield and want to refer to Lionel Blair. Type in your abbreviation and your new version of what you want Word to insert, in this case Lionel Blair. AutoCorrect will find the original entry and highlight it. The **Replace** button will appear – so press that.

Word does like to make sure you mean to do it when you change something, so you'll get another little dialogue box asking if you do want to redefine this AutoCorrect entry. Press **Yes** (if you do). And there you go: **Liz Broomfield** has changed into **Lionel Blair** (for example).

For all of the screen shots for this article, please see the original post on my blog.[5]

---

[5] www.libroediting.com/2012/06/13/autocorrect-in-word-2/

TOOLS 3: HOW TO HELP YOUR CLIENTS TO RECORD THEIR INTERVIEWS

Over the years I've been transcribing, I've found that my clients haven't always been as au fait as you would expect with recording, downloading and sending audio files of their interviews. Here are some handy hints that I've developed to help my clients – yours might find them useful, too.

Recording your interviews

You might be using a dedicated dictation machine or your Smartphone to record your interviews. Whichever you are using, here are some hints to get the best out of your recording:

Set and test the recording levels. You will probably be able to alter the volume, at very least, and maybe the graphic equaliser. If you're going to be doing a lot of interviews, it's worth doing a test session with a friend, and checking the quality of the recording. Then leave the levels set at that point.

> If the levels are too loud, when it's played back, it will be distorted, even if the level is turned down on the machine that's playing it back.

> If the levels are too quiet, when it's played back it will be really quiet still. Your transcriber will strain to hear it. Even if they up the volume at your end, there's only a certain amount they can do

> If the bass or treble are set too high, the recording will pick up and amplify all bass or treble noises, such as cars going past or cutlery rattling

You may have some pre-set recording levels in the menus on your recording device. Oddly enough, you need to choose one that reads something like "interview" or "one to one", rather than "meeting" or "concert" or "outdoors". This will ensure that the device picks up you and the interviewee, rather than the conversation at the next table or the inexorable whoosh of the cappuccino machine.

> If an inappropriate pre-set recording level is chosen, your transcriber may be bombarded with cutlery and glassware sounds and other people's conversations, or just hear voices booming around like they're in the bottom of a bucket.

> Check each time that the recording level is correct – it is not unknown for the buttons on the recording device to get pressed in the journalist's bag on the way to an interview, leading to a transcriber with ear-strain and a transcription full of gaps!

Transferring your audio files to your computer

Once you've saved your interview files, you're going to need to get them off your recording device and onto your computer.

There are usually two ways to do this:

Option 1 – connect your recording device to your computer using a USB cable

Option 2 – send the file from your recording device to your computer via email

Option 1 is the easiest. If your recording device comes with a USB connection, plug it in to your computer. You will find that the computer treats it as an extra drive, like the C or D drive. Use the file navigator to find the file and copy it across to your computer, ready to send to your transcriber.

Option 2 is more tricky, as most phones will have a limit as to how long a file you can send. You may need to break it up into chunks, or zip the file on your phone / dictation machine first.

There is an Option 3 which you can use if your dictation machine is an analogue one, i.e. uses those little tiny tapes (or big ones!). Go into a silent room. Set a microphone up connected to your computer. SET THE RECORDING LEVELS very carefully and test them. Play the tape and record it digitally. Note: please don't do this if you can help it. The tape quality will always be affected (think what the tapes were like that you recorded off the radio as a teenager. Exactly). Your Smartphone will have a voice memo app pre-loaded onto it, or you can download one. Do that: go digital. Your transcriber will thank you!

When your iPhone memo is too big to email ...

This is a topic in itself and one I've been asked about time and again.

If you need to transfer an iPhone voice memo to your computer to send to your transcriber, and you try to email it to yourself or them, you will probably get a message telling you that it's too long to email. Don't break it up into chunks, do this instead …

Turn on your phone, connect it via USB cable to your computer and open iTunes.

iTunes should have a tab called My iPhone. Click on the Sync button in this tab if it doesn't do it automatically. It will then record it into your computer's memory.

Under Playlists, click on Voice Memos. Find your recording (it will be labelled with its date, which should help you to find it), right-click and choose Get Info. This will tell you where the memo is saved on your computer. Copy it into the file where you want to keep it, and send it to your transcriber.

For other phones, I always recommend connecting the phone to the computer rather than trying to email it.

Sending your audio file to your transcriber

Most audio files are really big and won't send easily

as an email attachment.

The first thing to try is zipping it. Go to the file in your computer's folders, and right-click. You should be given some kind of option to Zip the file. This makes it smaller, like putting a duvet in one of those vacuum pack bags. Your transcriber will unzip it at their end to work with it.

If this is still too big, there are lots of services online that will transfer your file for you. My two favourites are YouSendIt, now called Hightail,[6] and Wetransfer.[7] Both of these have free versions – you pay more to get more feedback and send larger files.

You can also use Dropbox,[8] which acts as an extra, secure drive for your computer, living out there in the 'Cloud'. Sign up (again, free) and copy your files into this folder. Then share it with your transcriber, or send the file so they can download it.

If you want to share this information with your journalist or researcher clients, you can find it online.[9]

---

[6] www.hightail.com

[7] www.wetransfer.com

[8] www.dropbox.com

[9] www.libroediting.com/2013/12/18/how-to-record-transfer-and-send-audio-files-for-journalists-and-researchers/

TOOLS 4: RSI, ERGONOMICS AND KEYBOARDS

When you're a transcriber, you're going to, of necessity, end up working at a desk for long periods of time, using a keyboard. This can lead to problems with your posture, and possibly to RSI.

There are loads of different arguments and positions with regard to the ideal workstation position. So I'm just going to give a summary of what I've found to be good myself, and some of the ideas that are around, too. The best thing to do is:

> BE AWARE – keep an eye on how you're sitting, how you're feeling, and any aches, pains or niggles.

Typing position

This is what suits me: the old-fashioned way I was taught at Pitman typing college back in the early 90s: back straight, knees at 90 degrees, feet flat on the floor or a footrest. Shoulders relaxed, elbows at 90 degrees, belly button a hand-span away from the front of the keyboard, hands hovering OVER the keyboard so your wrists are straight and your fingers drop down onto the keys. Eyes aligned with the top of the monitor.

However, recent research that I've seen has suggested that you should lean back in your chair rather than sitting upright. I'm an upright sitter anyway (years of pony riding as a child?) so I find this uncomfortable.

There is also a lot of talk about standing desks, and I have several colleagues who have adopted these to great effect. I did try this and it made my feet hurt and made me type less quickly, so I did abandon it, but it's worth trying.

A note on laptops: laptop keyboards are really not suitable for large amounts of typing. They are very flat, even if propped up, and can really strain the hands and wrists. If you need to use a laptop as a computer, buy a plug-in keyboard to use in front of it.

Preventing RSI

The best ways to prevent RSI and other aches and pains are …

> Be aware of any problems when they start

> Be aware of your position at the desk (are you contorted or twisted? That's never good)

> Stretch and refocus every hour at least – move away from the desk, squat, stretch UP, stretch DOWN, walk up and down the stairs, do some squats

> Exercise regularly outside the house – I find that a good rowing session at the gym helps ease those shoulders

> If you get any suspicious pains, look at what you're doing and see if you can change it

> If you get a recurring pain, go to the doctor sooner rather than later

Your keyboard

Most people use the standard keyboard that came with their PC or Mac. That's fine for everyday use, but you might find the standard shape uncomfortable to use at high speeds, and the standard keyboard mechanics might slow down your typing. Here are some ideas:

Try one of the "ergonomic" split keyboards. They're split in half, with a hinge, so you can open or close them as you wish.

Try using an alternative key assignation. The most famous is "DVORAK" and you can find out about that quickly via its Wikipedia entry.[10] This assigns different letters to different keys, and is supposed to help with RSI issues by balancing how you type (we all know that the standard QWERTY keyboard was designed thus to stop the mechanics of the typewriter getting caught up with each other by putting commonly used pairs of letters in particular positions).

Try using a mechanical keyboard. Standard keyboards have a membrane under the keys which transmits the keystrokes to the switches. Their technology means that you have to press each key right down to get the connection and produce the letter. But mechanical keyboards have one individual mechanism and switch per key. You don't have to press them all the way down to produce the letter. They are much more

[10] www.en.wikipedia.org/wiki/Dvorak_Simplified_Keyboard

responsive and you can type more quickly on them, and they apparently last a lot longer – but they are expensive. I'm investing in one early this year, having tested lots of them.

A note on keyboard labels: If you type a lot, you will notice that the letter labels wear off your keys, especially the most heavily used ones. This seems fine if you're a touch typist anyway (and has the added benefit of really annoying anyone else who tries to use your workstation) but is irritating if you have to look down to type in passwords, etc.

The problem arises because most keyboards have the letters and numbers applied via transfer, which can wear off. You can get keyboards where the letter is actually moulded through each key, like a stick of rock. Wear your key down all you like, and the letter will still be there. Something worth looking into if you do wear off the letters on keyboards. You can even get light-up keyboards for when you want to type in the dark …

I'd suggest having a play with different types of keyboard at an office or computer supplies shop, especially when it comes to the more expensive mechanical type keyboards. Whatever you feel comfortable with and doesn't produce any aches or pains after a week of eight-hour days typing is what you should stick with, whether you're standing on your head or using some kind of odd keyboard that you invented. RSI can ruin your career and your health, so do take it seriously.

APPENDICES: WORKING AS A FREELANCER

Most transcribers are freelancers. In these appendices, I discuss how to check whether you're suited for a freelance career and how to set yourself up. Note that some of the advice is specific to the UK, but can be adapted for your home country – simply contact the body responsible for taxes in your region and you'll be all set.

APPENDIX 1: SETTING UP AS A FREELANCER

In August 2009 I decided to take what I'd been doing for people for free, as a kind of slightly odd hobby (in my case proofreading and editing) and turn it into a business. I didn't think I could sustain myself on a couple of one-off clients and a dream, so I "soft-launched", which means starting a business while having another income stream, in my case a day job I was doing already. I have learned a lot and I've been sharing this experience with other people starting small businesses at Social Media Cafes and Entrepreneur Meet-ups, so I thought I'd share it here, too. This is going to be a two-part series, with next week's post telling you what to do once you've set yourself up. But let's see whether this is the career choice for you, first!

Before you start

There are quite a few things it's worth thinking about before you launch yourself into a freelance career. Here are some of the main ones:

• **Do I have useful skills that people are prepared to pay for**? If you're already doing something in your daily work life that you would like to do on your own, then yes, you may well have (but see below warnings about doing the same thing for an employer and yourself).   If you've just got a general idea about going into business for yourself, think about skills you have developed as part of your job or a hobby. I had done a fair bit of editing and writing in various jobs, but it didn't strike me how many different things I could offer until I was running the business. I could have offered more from the very beginning.

• **Is there a market for my particular skills**, and will I be able to access it? If you're experienced in a particular area, do you have contacts who will help you find freelance work? Contacts are the key. Are there companies who might take a sample, for example shops which might stock your knitted widgets or people who might share a stand at a craft fair. Think about specialist skills you might have –

for example, I have experience working for the UK office of an American company, so I'm able to offer localisation services changing US into UK English.

• **Can I work from home on my own?** Most freelance jobs do involve a fair bit of working alone. Even a photographer or someone who sells through a market stall will need to spend a fair amount of marketing and admin time alone. Are you good at motivating yourself? If you need people around you – well, co-working spaces can be very useful, but there is still a fair bit of sitting in your house pondering, doing admin, and getting on with work.

• **How will this affect the rest of my life?** This is ever so important if you're thinking of starting your own business while still working. As I said at the beginning, that's how I've done it, and there have been times when I've had so much of my own work that I've had to put off friends, tell my partner he can only spend time with me if he sits in the chair in my study … silently! and I've pretty much given up reading for pleasure. Can your social and family life take this? Make sure you have your partner and/or family's support.

Early days

Once you've answered these questions and decided to set up on your own, I advise doing the following:

- Getting yourself **online**: it's wise to get hold of a domain name right away (the URL of your website will be http://www.libroediting.com and not http://www.libroediting.wordpress.com for example), and set up a web page and email addresses using it. It is generally agreed that you look more professional if you do this. And the more professional you appear to be, the more business you will attract.

- If you're in the UK, go on the **HMRC** course "Becoming self-employed"[11] (find information in your local library or on the HMRC website). This is my number one recommendation to people starting a business. The course leader will tell you what records to keep so you can do important things like your tax return, and they tell you all about what to do, what funding and special tax breaks you can get, etc.

- Again, in the UK, **register your business** with HMRC[12] – you have to do this within a certain period after you start working and being paid for it. Have a look on their website or give them a ring. Their staff have always been very friendly and helpful when I've called them.

- UK again – register for a **Certificate of Small**

---

[11] www.hmrc.gov.uk/bst/advice-team-events/work1.htm

[12] www.hmrc.gov.uk/selfemployed/

Earnings Exception – this allows you to earn a certain amount before paying National Insurance and tax.

• Get **business cards** – at first you can use somewhere inexpensive like Vistaprint but it's important to have something to give out to potential clients and people who might recommend you. Don't go for gimmicks, just business cards will do at the start.

• Be careful if you want to do as your own business something that you are already doing in your **day job**. You might be about to be made redundant. If so – use those skills. If you're going to do it part-time while still working in that area, make sure your employer is OK with that and check your contract – ditto if you leave to set up on your own. Better safe than sorry – and you will get found out.

APPENDIX 2: WORKING AS A FREELANCER

Right, so once you've gone through the questions I posed above and decided that you are suited to freelance work, and you've been on the initial courses that I recommended, it's time to set up good, reliable working practices right from the start. These are some things I've found handy:

• **Prioritise.** This is key. Make sure you have time for work, yourself and other people. If you work all hours, you'll run yourself into the ground. That won't do anyone any good. And if you are likely to end up doing lots of little projects …

• **Organise**. I set up a Gantt chart on a spreadsheet – clients down the side, dates along the top, and I colour-block in dates that projects are booked in for, changing the colour as they arrive, when I've invoiced, when they've paid. It's a really good way to see what you've got on and whether you can fit in that extra client project.

- Set up **terms and conditions**. I have standard email text that I sent out when I'm quoting for a job, stating when I will ask for payment, how they can pay, what I'm doing, etc. For larger ongoing clients, I set up an agreement in a Word document and make sure we've both agreed to it. It's better to know how you're going to end things or deal with conflicts before it comes to the crunch.

- **Invoice**. Make sure you invoice clients as soon as you've done the job. Or before, if you work that way round. If you arrange to invoice people for several projects at the end of the month, do it. There's software you can buy, or you can just set up a Word template. Then make sure you check and record their payment. That's where the Gantt chart comes in handy. Not in green – they haven't paid and it might be time to chase up.

- **Tools.** Make sure you have up to date and legitimate versions of the software you need – Word, etc. If you will be working with any kind of software, whether to read knitting patterns or invent widgets, there are often free downloads available, or trial copies.

- **Work for your clients, not yourself**. Some of my clients, like students and translators, need me to show all the changes in Track Changes so they make the decision on what to change and I'm not writing their work for them. Other clients just want me to go in, rewrite and send it back to them. Offer your clients choices, but be prepared to make recommendations based on what similar people have requested, too.
- Be **flexible and open**. I started off as an editor and proofreader. But as clients asked me to do more things, I added in writing, transcription, copy-typing and localising to my portfolio. All things I could actually do already! More income streams, more work! Have a think about what you can offer outside of your core products. If you knit toys, why not run a class or knit some funny shapes for adults. That came out a bit funny, but you know what I mean!
- **Network.** Both among your peers (in the business and other freelancers who work from home) and among other businesspeople in your area. Twitter and Facebook are useful for finding out what's going on. It gets you out of the house and meeting people. LinkedIn offers business networking online – join the groups and get chatting.
- **Outsource**. Know when you need help. If something is going to take you longer in terms of

hours and cost more in terms of work you can't do while you're doing a task, outsource it. Freelance journalist – get someone else to transcribe your tapes. Not good at sums – get a bookkeeper or accountant in to control your records. It's also useful to know people in the same line of business as you to whom you can pass work in an emergency. I hope you find these handy hints useful. I've grown in confidence and developed my skills and, not a natural entrepreneur, have built a successful and flourishing business!

APPENDIX 3: HOW DO I GET FREELANCE WORK?

This article shares some ways that I've found successful in getting transcribing work. It's applicable to getting freelance work with individuals and companies, rather than full-time employed job in publishing, etc.

It's also worth noting here, in response to some of the early comments on here, that this is a suite of options and you wouldn't expect to do them all at the same time. Once you've built up 1 and 2, you can pick and choose depending on what your career path is – and it's important to indulge in some planning from the start.

1. Make sure that you say what you do on your website

Many of your clients will come to you after doing a Google search. Remember: people will take the easy option. Why bother to search on lists and in directories if you can just stick a search in Google.

So it's worth making sure that your website …

Includes a clear list of all of the services you offer

Includes a blog which is updated regularly – this really helps your position on the search results

Is Search Engine Optimised in general (there is an art to this, but make sure you include your keywords regularly, write lots of natural reading text and include keywords in page / post titles and headings)

Includes a picture of you and ways to contact you – a contact form is always good for this

Oh yes – do make sure that you HAVE a website. Even if it's just one page, I really do think that in all industries, from carpentry to computer programming, people expect you to have some kind of web presence, and may well give up the search there and then if you don't, even if you've been recommended by name by someone. I know that I do that when I'm looking for services …

2. Make sure that people know what you do

An awful lot of my early clients came through friends of friends and social networks. Obviously, don't bombard your friends by begging them to refer you, but make sure the following are covered:

If you have a company Facebook page, include a list of your services

Include your services on your Twitter profile

Mention what you do on social networks every now and again (a good way to do this is to mention what you've BEEN doing "This month I've transcribed interviews for some music journalists and a focus group".

Make sure peers in one area know you cover other areas, too (if you do), e.g. I make sure that my editing chums know that I transcribe as well

Consider setting up a newsletter and making sure you mention all of your services

Update your clients with any new services you're offering

3. Join industry groups and publicise yourself through their directories

I gained early clients through being in a member

directory associated with a copyeditors' email list. There are transcribers' groups and some do have directories. All of these are places where people will look for accredited and proved suppliers.

4. Advertise on general directories and websites

A hint: don't bother with paid ones when there are so many free directories and websites!

Ask around your peers as to what they find useful. I am on Freeindex and get a few enquiries a month. Join as many as you want, but do make sure to update your profile if you change your services, fees, etc.

Local print directories and especially business association directories can be good. I have a free listing in our local business association one, which has never brought me any work, but I always try to find local tradespeople who are members, and other people will do this, too.

5. Use industry-specific freelancer sites

I've had a look at general websites like freelancer.com and oDesk and personally, I don't think they're worth it. A lot of people on those will undercut and take any job at the lowest price possible. Many of the sites have "tests" which are actually a test of your understanding of the site itself, not your ability as a writer, editor or whatever. I have been informed that, of these sites, Elance.com is the best of the bunch, and does have reasonably paid transcription jobs listings.

However, there are industry-specific freelancer sites which are worth it. Again, ask your peers for recommendations. The one that's got me the most work is proz.com, which is a site for translators where you can put up a profile and, if you pay for membership, that profile will be sent to people looking for freelancers, and they will contact you direct. This has paid back the membership fee for me tens of times over, because I work with translators into English, and offer localisation, which is related to translation.

You can also look for people looking for particular skills and freelancers and then pitch to them.

Take note, though: with anything you pay for, do assess each year whether you've got that fee back, and more. Only continue paying if you're getting a good return on your investment!

6. Advertise (selectively)

I'm not a big fan of paying out for adverts. Most of the other methods I talk about here are free. But there might be specific advertising channels that will work for you.

When I was starting out, working as a proofreader on theses and dissertations, I put up some posters around the university where I worked, recruiting colleagues who were also students to put them up in common rooms, etc. (free, except for printing costs and a few coffees!) and I advertised in the university staff newsletter, which went to tutors and supervisors. The costs were low, even to non-staff, and I did get the money back. This is something you could consider for transcription work if you're targeting

As with using websites that you pay for, do check your return on investment and keep an eye on the outgoings.

7. Use social media proactively

This one particularly applies to Twitter, although LinkedIn can be used in this way, too. Search for people looking for your services on Twitter. Reach out to potential clients directly. I have got paid work using this method and, even better (see below), I've got clients who have gone on to be big recommenders this way, too.

No one minds one, polite Tweet if they've asked for recommendations for a good transcriber and you fit the bill. Don't hassle people and don't blanket-tweet; do tailor your response to the person you're contacting.

8. Seek recommendations and referrals from clients

The best way to get new clients is through word of mouth. The two main advantages?

It's free!

If person A recommends you to person B, and person B gets in touch with you, they are far more likely to convert into a paying customer than someone who's randomly got in touch with you through an ad or Google search.

You do need to be a bit proactive about this, though …

Make sure that your clients know you're looking for more clients just like them

Say thank you whenever you find out someone's recommended you

Ask clients for references to put on a reference page on your website (this makes enquirers more likely to use you as you come recommended by lots of people)

I have several clients who act as "nodes" for me, recommending me either individually or via blog posts and pages on their websites.

8. Seek recommendations from your peers

Your peers fall into two groups:

People who freelance or run small businesses like you, who you might meet in online groups or at networking events

People in the same industry as you, who you might meet in the same ways

It's important not to see people in the same industry as you as competitors – you're much better off considering one another as colleagues. When I was starting out, I was passed what turned out to be a major client by a friend who wanted to stop working at weekends and in the evenings. So I did evening and weekend cover for them. Now I'm established, I much prefer to be able to recommend potential clients who I can't take on to another qualified person who I know will do a good job.

When you're starting out, it's worth forging (genuine) relationships with people in your industry who are more established. They may well have the odd customer they want to pass on, or have too much business and be looking for people to recommend on to. Nowadays, I pass quite a few people who I can't accommodate on to a core set of five or so recommended proofreaders, writers and transcribers. I also keep a note of people in allied industries, so I can pass people to them with a relevant recommendation, rather than just leaving them hanging.

I haven't got many clients directly through networking, but I met an author at an event who went on to recommend my transcription services to a fellow author, who now uses me for transcription and editing, AND recommends me on her website!

8. Give cold calling a go

Some people do cold calling, where they literally call people on the phone and ask them for work. Personally, I feel this takes a LOT of investment. Cold calling requires a list, which takes time and research or money to get. It might be more worth looking at trade directories or local directories before you take this path.

However, cold calling can be useful if you're

targeting a specific and maybe narrow group of clients. If there's a group of companies that you can identify as a good fit, by all means approach them with a call or letter, cold, as it were.

CONCLUSION: OFF YOU GO!

I hope this guide has helped to give you an insight into the job of being a transcriber and how to go about checking it's for you and setting yourself up. As well as specific information on transcription, I've shared some more general career-building advice as well.

If you want more general advice, please do take a look at my other, longer books, How I Survived my First Year of Full-Time Self-Employment: Going it Alone at 40 and Running a Successful Business after the Start-Up Phase: Who are you Calling Mature? More information can be found here on my website at www.lizbroomfieldbooks.com, and these are suitable for readers in all areas of freelancing and the small business world.

I would be very grateful if you could share a review of this guide on whichever online book store you bought it from. This really helps me to share advice and support with as many people as possible. I'm passionate about sharing the lessons that I've learned and giving as much information to as wide an audience as I can.

Do get in touch and let me know what you thought of this guide – you can visit one of my websites and find the contact forms or of course email me at liz@libroediting.com.

ABOUT THE AUTHOR

Liz Broomfield (the pen name of Liz Dexter) is an editor, transcriber, proofreader and localiser based in Birmingham, UK. She's passionate about sharing the lessons she's learned as someone who changed careers mid-life and is living a flexible and happy life doing work she loves, with time for the other things she loves in life.

Liz's books can be found on Amazon, Smashwords and Selz in print and all formats of e-book.

Visit Liz's book website at
www.lizbroomfieldbooks.com

Visit Liz's business and Word tips website at
www.libroediting.com

ABOUT MY BOOKS

I write books that help self-employed people and people setting up and running small businesses to work out what to do first and what to do next. I write from my own experience, using lots of examples from my successful business life, and my books are all jargon-free, approachable and friendly. Most importantly, if you buy the book, you get the information that's promised. There's no requirement to buy a course or pay for additional materials. In fact, links and footnotes will take you to more FREE resources on my websites with screen shots and the latest updates. Find information, news and links to buy at www.lizbroomfieldbooks.com. Happy reading!

"How I Survived my First Year of Full-Time Self-Employment: Going it Alone at 40" – all you need to know about setting up your new business and taking the plunge without too much risk or anxiety. Lots of personal stories and I share exactly how I did it – you don't need to buy any courses or additional resources to get the full value from this book.

"Running a Successful Business after the Start-up Phase or, Who are you Calling Mature?" – you've set up the business, you've been running for a couple of years, now it's time to refine your customer base, redress your work-life balance and think about add-ons like social media networking and blogging. This book tells you how and like its predecessor, shares real-life examples which show exactly how I've built a happy self-employed life for myself.

The business OMNIBUS "Your Guide to Starting and Building your Business" – why not save money on buying the above two books separately with this e-only guide to setting up and maintaining a successful and balanced business? I do like to provide value to my readers, and this includes the text of both books in full, put together in a special omnibus edition. It's downloadable in all of the different e-book formats or as a pdf to read on your computer or tablet.

"Quick Guide to Networking, Social Media and Social Capital" takes you through the benefits you can gain – and give – when you engage with people through face-to-face or social networking.

"How I Conquered High Cholesterol Through Diet and Exercise" – my first e-book and still one of the most popular, this takes you through what high cholesterol means, which foods make it worse and which might improve it, and places you might like to try eating, including restaurant tips for the UK and US. Built from my own experience, this offers an option for reducing cholesterol without drugs.

Printed in Great Britain
by Amazon